WORLD'S FIRST 'SELFIE'

THE BEST OF

MATT

2014

MATTHEW PRITCHETT

studied at St Martin's School of Art in London and first saw himself published in the *New Statesman* during one of its rare lapses from high seriousness. He has been the *Daily Telegraph*'s front-page pocket cartoonist since 1988. In 1995, 1996, 1999, 2005, 2009 and 2013 he was the winner of the Cartoon Arts Trust Award and in 1991, 2004 and 2006 he was 'What the Papers Say' Cartoonist of the Year. In 1996, 1998, 2000, 2008 and 2009 he was the *UK Press Gazette* Cartoonist of the Year and in 2002 he received an MBE.

Own your favourite Matt cartoons. Browse the full range of Matt cartoons and buy online at www.telegraph.co.uk/photographs or call 020 7931 2076.

'There are three of us
in this cinema'

The Daily Telegraph

THE BEST OF

MATT

2014

An Orion Paperback

First published in Great Britain in 2014 by Orion Books
A division of the Orion Publishing Group Ltd
Orion House
5 Upper Saint Martin's Lane
London, WC2H 9EA

A Hachette UK Company

10 9 8 7 6 5 4 3 2 1

A CIP catalogue record for this book
is available from the British Library.

ISBN: 978 1 4091 4817 3

Printed in the UK by CPI William Clowes, Beccles NR34 7TL

The Orion Publishing Group's policy is to use papers that
are natural, renewable and recyclable products and
made from wood grown in sustainable forests. The logging
and manufacturing processes are expected to conform to
the environmental regulations of the country of origin.

www.orionbooks.co.uk

'It was his last wish'

THE BEST OF

MATT

2014

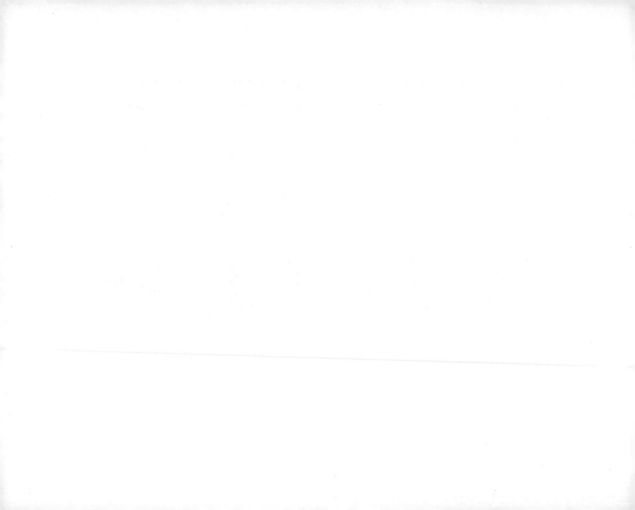

'I'm quitting Dry January'

'I'm just going to scrape
the barnacles off the car'

Floods and Gales

'We've had a month's worth
of abuse in less than 24 hours'

'I'm a castaway. I've been
adrift for months on the
Somerset Levels'

'You're not smoking in
there, are you?'

No Smoking
in Cars with Children

Roses are red
They sell them in shops
My love is like the rain
It never bloody stops

'Our roof was photographed
on the A303 doing 85 mph'

'There was a gust of wind
and we lost 12 models'

'I have to go back to the office. I can't remember if I turned off the money'

'If you live near an energy boss, pop in and check he's not trapped under his wallet'

'I love this time of year – crisp
mornings, autumn colours
and gigantic price rises'

'Don't restore the power,
I'm saving a fortune'

'Our steaks are aged for 28 days and cooked with gas from the most expensive energy providers'

'I opened our gas bill and the canary fainted'

'Do you have any candles
that can charge an iPhone?'

House Prices

'Do you still want to look
round the house? You're
already £25,000 late'

'The minute we heard about
the housing bubble we
rushed out to buy one'

'You fainted when I told you the price. I'm afraid while you were unconscious it went up another £5,000'

'We'll take it'

Education

'Coalition infighting is getting worse. Mr Gove has had his lunch money stolen'

'It's a miracle! The image of Nick Clegg has appeared in my mashed potato'

'I don't know if my phone
battery will last that long'

'Miss Roberts will be in
charge of sex education ...'

Education

'They've made the
GCSE results envelope
much harder to open'

'The relentless grade inflation
has finally been halted'

'And don't be late tomorrow, it's the school photo ...'

'Wait till I catch that cat ...'

'I don't have any halal chicken, but I've got a packet of agnostic sausages'

'Either I have a wobbly wheel, or my trolley is trying to face Mecca'

'I will now be locked into a bad
pension deal and dropped
in a tank of water'

'I can't decide whether to
buy an annuity or blow the
lot on a bag of crisps'

New rules

Pensions

Labour plans

'When you said you were taking me out for the evening I wasn't expecting a flu jab'

Surgeries open longer hours

'Ooh, that looks nasty. I'll get someone to kiss it better'

'I don't know how they
got past the receptionist'

'The contenders are:
the Police Crime Figures and
the NHS Waiting Times'

'Our new boss used to
run an open prison. We're
currently missing two tigers,
a lion and a crocodile'

'He says it's half past two,
but he's probably lying'

'I voted UKIP. Well, to be
honest, I paid a Bulgarian
to go and do it for me'

'We've bought the beer and
we've bought the fags ...
we're pretty much done'

'I was middle class till
Ed Miliband "saved" me'

Teenage Runaways

'Our pupils go on many
foreign trips – some of them
arranged by the school'

'The parents should treasure
this time. Soon their children
will have grown up and
moved back in with them'

'Tsvetelina, after that, I want you to write a speech for me on immigration control'

'I don't want Bulgarians and Romanians coming over here taking jobs away from the Poles'

Scottish Independence

'It's UK oil until it spills on to a beach and then it's Scottish oil'

GLASGOW FISH

SPECIAL

MARS BAR & CHIPS—

THE BATTERED TOGETHER CAMPAIGN

'I wouldn't say that was triple A status'

'Are you seeing someone else?'

Hollande visits mistress on scooter

Health Advice

'When I hired you to kill my husband I didn't expect you to come and cook him steak every day'

'Be careful, I've heard these music festivals are rife with fruit juices and sugary drinks'

'A pint of bitter – and put
a cherry in it'

'He was trying to get his
statins out of the bin'

Health

'Wrong leg? Apart from that, would you describe yourself as completely satisfied?'

'Since it bit you, this mosquito seems a lot older and more forgetful'

'He painted people in the
North looking worried
about fracking'

'I've developed a parsnip that
can frack for shale gas'

Match Fixing

'If you want daddy to lose on purpose, you'll have to pay me £7,000'

'Bye, luv, have a good draw'

'That's four penalty points
to Princess Anne for
inappropriate use
of the knife and fork'

Horsemeat debate

Co-op

'You might worry less about my overdraft if you took some crack cocaine'

'We should probably get that sorted out too'

'Cancel all holiday. We're doubling production'

'Grant Shapps in a fix – 66'

Budget for Bingo and Beer

Summer of Sport

'You're about to have a
very painful lesson
in Englishness'

Referees' foam

'We shouldn't become involved in any more World Cups – it always ends in disaster'

'Come to the front of the queue if you can play cricket'

Summer of Sport

'One day of biting is followed by four months of fasting'

'I was going to watch Suarez play at Barcelona, but I'm far too squeamish'

Suarez in trouble

'The Germans have been very rude to the hosts. The England team would never do that'

Germany 7 Brazil 1

Summer of Sport

'Come on, Andy,
BITE HIM'

'One day soon we'll develop
a resistance to sporting
disasters and become immune'

Over-use of antibiotics

'And we've just heard that six riders have tested positive for Wensleydale cheese'

'Typical, 200 cyclists and not one of them stops at a red light'

Summer of Sport

'Scottish and Commonwealth
athletes get their medals
free, but the English
have to pay'

'Is this judo, or a discussion
about keeping the £ ?'

'He'd travelled to Wimbledon where fanatics brainwashed him into becoming a ball boy'

Royal horse tested positive

'A quick pint? I'll check with my wife – she wears the mitre in this house'

'Maybe it will be a bishop or a Cabinet Minister, or perhaps it's just a boy'

'I think the men should
leave us now while
we discuss politics'

'Does my Ministerial
portfolio look big in this?'

Foreign Affairs

Commemorations

'Putin's here.
Everybody ignore him'

'Hello, Eurovision. Here are
the results from Russia...
Ukraine–nul points'

'It gives off so much heat
and it runs entirely on
election pledges'

'My Government will throw
scrunched up balls of paper
into the bin and stare out of
the window until the election'

'Lovely service, vicar,
but I think you should
leave God to the politicians'

'It's a threatening note
tied to a sandal'

Cameron does God

Europe

'If you can't beat him,
join him'

'Whatever you do, don't
agree to settle this with a
penalty shoot-out'

UK fails to block new EC President

Trojan Horse

'It says you're impossible
to radicalise and you fail
to grasp even the basics
of extremism'

'Getting you to vault a
horse doesn't make this a
terrorist training camp'

'I knew they migrated,
but I had no idea they
did security checks'

'This is your mother. Airport
security want to know why
you never phoned me'

'Some time ago I lent you
my ladder. You now owe
me 236 ladders'

'We're not actually IN profit,
but we're a short 150-mile
cab ride from it'

'I bought this 5p carrier bag
before Christmas and I'd
like to return it'

'I'm not actually a worker
ant. I'm only doing this so
I don't lose my benefits'

'Travel in the front four
coaches. There will be a
"conscious uncoupling"
after South Croydon'

'Will sir be wearing his
formal, evening balaclava?'

'Will you ask the witness
how she gets her chocolate
cake so wonderfully moist?'

'This year I'm doing a
Nigella Christmas'

Delays

'Typical! The one day the escalator is working there's a tube strike'

'I'm inquiring about HS2 train times. They've put me on hold'

First trains by 2025

'We got pet passports for
the children. It was
much quicker'

'There's a 6 to 8 week wait for
a Father's Day card unless
you pay a £55 priority fee'

Climate change?

'...hot weather safety leaflet
...hot weather safety leaflet...'

'If the lightning hits
the barbecue it might
cook the sausages'

'Would I get more presents
if you scrapped all
the green crap?'

Climate change?

'These goal celebrations are getting out of control'

Anelka quenelle gesture

'Can Johnny come out? I've sold him to a Spanish football club'

Gareth Bale

And finally...

'We've ditched the £ and adopted fudge as our official currency'

Cornwall recognised as Celtic minority

'We should give Tony Benn a State funeral – it would have really annoyed him'

'Let me guess – you've become
a Royal Mail shareholder'

'The Heathrow expansion
came closer than we expected'

And finally...

And finally...

'Three kings are coming with gold, frankincense and myrrh. I listened to their voicemails'

Hacking trial

'We've taken up smoking so we don't have to chauffeur you around'

'And can you point to the man who refused to buy you a pony?'

Emotional cruelty

And finally…

BBC pay-off

'It's to stop him watching the 50 Shades of Grey trailer'

'SIT DOWN'

And finally...

And finally...

'Do you realise that if we sold our house we could afford to heat it?'

'Would you like one of our plastic carrier bags? The price has gone up to £5,000'

'I live in the country and
when I'm in London I stay
at my drunk tank'

Binge drinking

'HMS Victory made out
of matches. You may be
England's biggest shipbuilder'

'It's been in the family
for generations. The
Nazis refused to loot it'

Stolen art

'I heard it cough'

TB from cats

'I'm sorry, this has never
happened to me before'

And finally…

And finally...

Bob Crow

'I thought I was putting money into ISAs'